# The City of
# YORK

R W HORTON

FRONT COVER: *Bootham Bar dominates the road from the north, the direction from which in the Middle Ages the city could expect its most dangerous enemies. It stands on the site of one of the Roman entrances to Eboracum. The portcullis is still to be seen in the bar.*

RIGHT: *York Minster, riding high above a patchwork of roofs, towers and spires, dominates the city. The gardens of the Royal York Hotel make a colourful foreground to the Minster.*

BACK COVER: *The north side of York Minster seen from Dean's Park.*

# THE CITY OF YORK

YORK is the capital of the north country and the second city of the realm. It lies at the junction of the rivers Ouse and Foss where the Romans built their first fortification in A.D. 71 and named it Eboracum.

The city is encompassed by its medieval walls, over which the Minster of St. Peter stands sentinel. The history of York is the history of England and every episode in its development reads like an adventure story.

Although the Romans planned the fortress in a most military and regular fashion, time has left an intricate web of streets and alleys where shafts of light and shadow play, where the upper storeys of buildings overhang until they nearly touch, where sudden, unexpected views appear of the Minster, a court yard or a tree in blossom.

It is a city with fine traditions in scholarship, music, arts and crafts. York has always been at the forefront of activity; once a Roman outpost, then a cradle of early Christianity, a centre of progressive education, sometimes a bulwark against invading hordes, sometimes even the base for the invader, a capital city and for a time the seat of government.

The names of the streets often reflect the trades or activities which were carried out there. The lovely old street of Stonegate, for instance, was given its name because of the stone which was transported along it for use in the construction of the pre-Norman Minster.

The city is proud of its Minster, its

civic buildings and treasures, and also of the fact that the Lord Mayor of York is second only in rank to the Lord Mayor of London.

Although there is a story which claims that York was founded by Ebraucus some 1000 years before Christ was born, the history of the city before the Romans is shrouded in the mists of time. There can be little doubt, however, that a settlement of Brigantes existed on or near the site chosen by the Romans on which to construct their fortress.

When the Romans again invaded Britain in A.D. 43 the land was divided into about 30 independent tribes. The most warlike of these was that of the Brigantes whose territory extended from Strathclyde down to the Humber and across to the Mersey. For some time Lincoln and Chester were the farthest outposts of Roman control, but on being proclaimed emperor, Vespasian's first objective was to subdue northern Britain and to do this he ordered Quintus Petillius Cerealis to take command of the forces intended to crush the Brigantes. The 9th Legion, stationed at Lincoln, was selected to carry out this campaign and moved northwards under its commander. In A.D. 71 a defensive position was constructed where the rivers Ouse and Foss meet; this fort was named Eboracum and from here the Romans conducted their campaign against the north.

The *via principalis* or 'Main Street' of the fort, now Petergate, ran parallel to the front and rear defences. At each end of the road there was an entrance: the *porta principalis dextra* or 'Right Main Gate', now Bootham Bar, was one; the other, the *porta principalis*

\* \* \*

FACING PAGE: *Walmgate Bar with its barbican, which was constructed to protect this entrance to the city.*

ABOVE: *High Petergate follows the line of a Roman road, the* via principalis. *Originally it joined what is now Low Petergate at the* Praetorium *or headquarters where the Minster stands.*

BELOW: *Stonegate follows the line of a Roman way, the* via praetoria *which joined the* via principalis *at the* Praetorium. *Like Petergate the buildings date from medieval to Georgian times.*

*sinistra* or 'Left Main Gate' was located in King's Square. A road called the *via praetoria*, now Stonegate, was constructed from a position halfway along the *via principalis* and led to the main entrance of the camp; the *porta praetoria* was situated in what is now St. Helen's Square. A fourth opening, the *porta decumana*, was located in a position opposite to the main entrance. The *praetorium*, or 'Commander's Headquarters', was situated in the centre of the camp where the Minster now stands; the Market Place and the Provost's Quarters were situated to the right and left of the *praetorium* and on each side of the *via praetoria* were the barracks.

The early defences were probably constructed of earth mounds covered with turf. These were later surmounted with timber stockades, and it is unlikely that the walls were constructed before A.D. 100.

The next stage in the development of the walls occurred between 284 and 337 when polygonal bastions and intermediate towers were added. A Roman multangular tower can be seen in the Museum Gardens and the remains of another beyond Monk Bar by the side of the medieval walls. In the period between 343 and 370 earth ramparts were thrown up inside the walls and turrets were added.

The 9th Legion was based at Eboracum for some 50 years and it was probably due to a surprise attack on the camp that the Legion was completely annihilated. The Roman emperor Hadrian sent the 6th Legion from the Lower Rhine to deal with the situation and by building his famous wall from the Tyne to the Solway Firth he cut off the Brigantes from their Caledonia allies in Scotland. After this the Roman occupation settled down to a more peaceful routine.

The emperor Severus came to York in 208 and after two campaigns into Scotland he returned to Eboracum where he died. It was here, while looking at the urn which he knew would contain his ashes, that he said: "Thou shalt hold what the whole world could not contain". His body was burned on a huge pyre outside the city and his ashes were taken to Rome.

\* \* \*

ABOVE (left): *The church of St. Mary Bishophill. The tower contains some Roman masonry and its Saxon window with central baluster is of particular interest.*

ABOVE (right): *All Saints Church, North Street, dates from pre-Conquest times and contains some fine 14th- and 15th-century stained glass.*

FACING PAGE (above): *The medieval city walls on the south side of the river. The imposing Railway War Memorial is on the left.*

FACING PAGE (below): *The Multangular Tower in the Museum Gardens. It was built about A.D. 300 on the site of older defences. The upper stonework is medieval. Originally the tower formed the west corner of the Roman fort.*

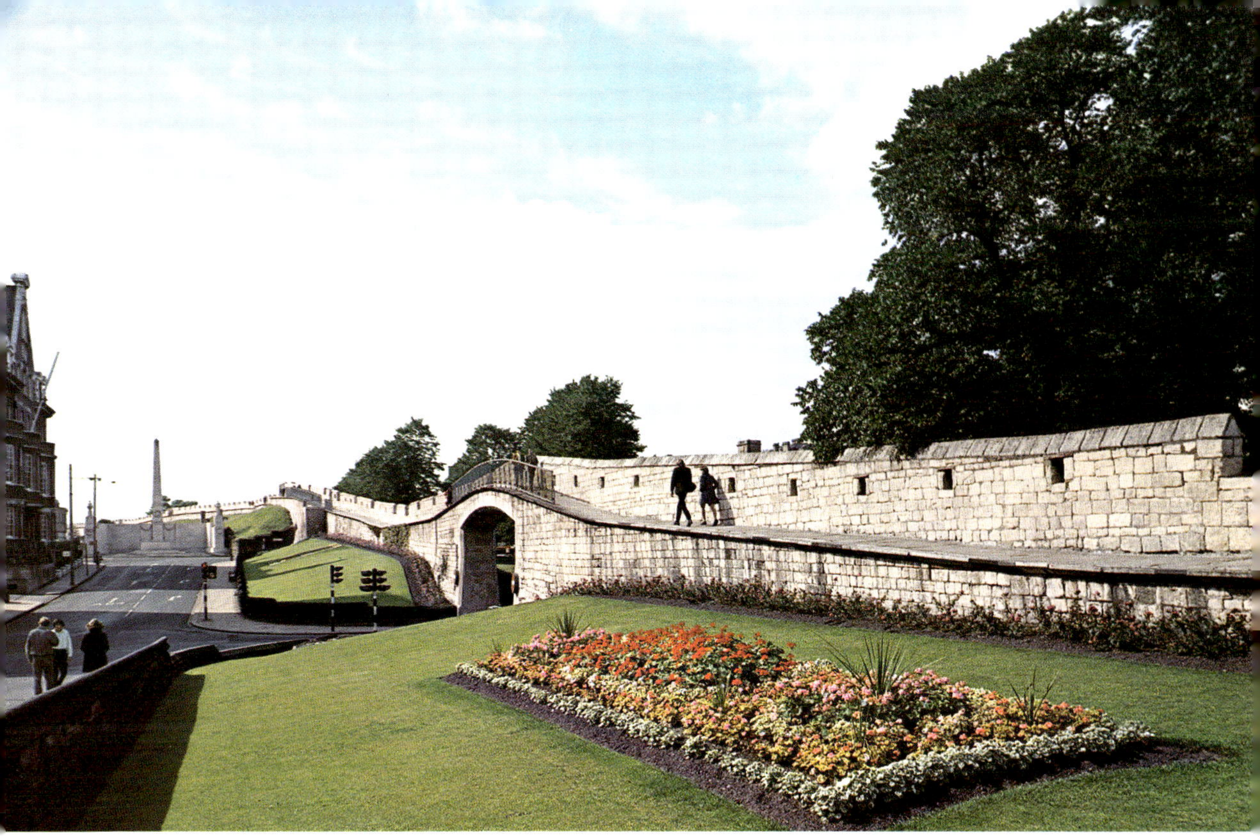

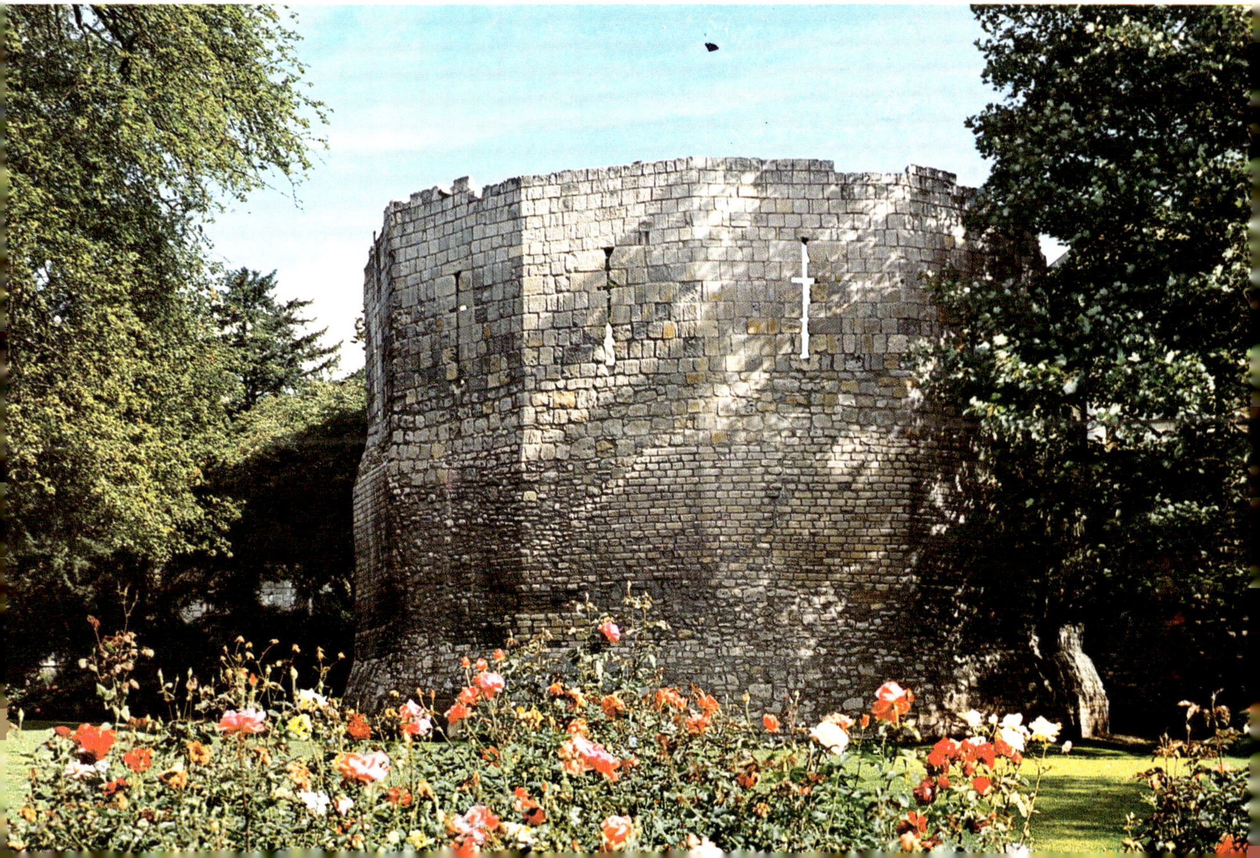

Under Constantius, Eboracum increased in importance and became the headquarters of civil and military government. When he died in 306, his son Constantine was proclaimed emperor in York. The city's links with Rome had thus become direct and powerful.

A year after Constantine issued his Edict of Toleration recognizing Christianity, he called the earliest council of the church at Arles in 314, and it is interesting to note that Eborius, bishop of Eboracum, was present.

During the later Roman period Eboracum was extended by the formation of a civil settlement at the south side of the fort and this settlement was probably the forerunner of Peasholme Green and St. Saviourgate.

Life in Eboracum was peaceful and prosperous at this period, but when the Romans were recalled to defend their own country from the Goths the Britons were left to protect themselves. What happened after 417 can only be conjectured, but when the Britons appealed to the Romans for help in 446 none was forthcoming.

The effect of Roman influence lasted for some years but later much of the country sank into barbarism. During the fifth and sixth centuries the history of Eboracum, and for that matter the rest of the country, is obscure.

When the Angles took the city in about 560 they probably found the Roman walls in good order and it was about this time that the city was extended in a westerly direction.

The country about York, and as far north as the Cleveland Hills, was called Deira and the first known king of the territory was Ella. Some four years after the birth of his son, Edwin, king Ella died and Deira was seized by the king of Bernicia. In 616 Edwin, who was then some 30 years old, persuaded Redwald of East Anglia to help him regain his kingdom; this he did and after a great battle a year later Edwin became king of all Northumbria.

Soon afterwards Edwin wished to take as his wife Ethelburga, the daughter of Ethelbert the Christian king of Kent, and he was only permitted to do so on the understanding that Ethelburga was allowed to worship as she wished. The princess and Edwin came north and with them came a monk named Paulinus who had recently been ordained bishop at Canterbury. Ethelburga and Edwin were married in 625 and two years later a small timber church was erected on or near the site of the Roman *praetorium*, where king Edwin was baptized by Paulinus. From this beginning rose the Minster.

War broke out once again and when Edwin was killed in battle at Hatfield, York was taken by the victor, Cadwalla. Edwin's queen and her children were escorted back to Kent by Paulinus while another monk, James the Deacon, remained in the hostile north to teach and baptize.

The first raids of the dreaded Vikings—the Danish 'men of the harbours'—were spasmodic, but in the winter of 866 a great horde of them took up quarters in East Anglia. Civil war broke out in Northumbria and during this time the Danes attacked and took York or Eoforwic as the city was by this time called. The two Northumbrian leaders settled their quarrel and with their followers tried to recapture the city but in the violent battle that followed both were killed. The remainder made peace and the Anglian kingdom never recovered. After taking York, the Danes went

\* \* \*

RIGHT: *Fishergate Postern, part of Fishergate Tower which is the only tower to have retained its postern gate.*

FACING PAGE: *The hall of the Merchant Adventurers of York, a gild founded about 1356. In the 15th and 16th centuries the gild was the undisputed ruler of the city. The hall, which dates from 1365, has an undercroft, a chapel and a magnificent timbered roof which is seen below. Up to the 19th century the undercroft contained the Hospital of the Holy Trinity.*

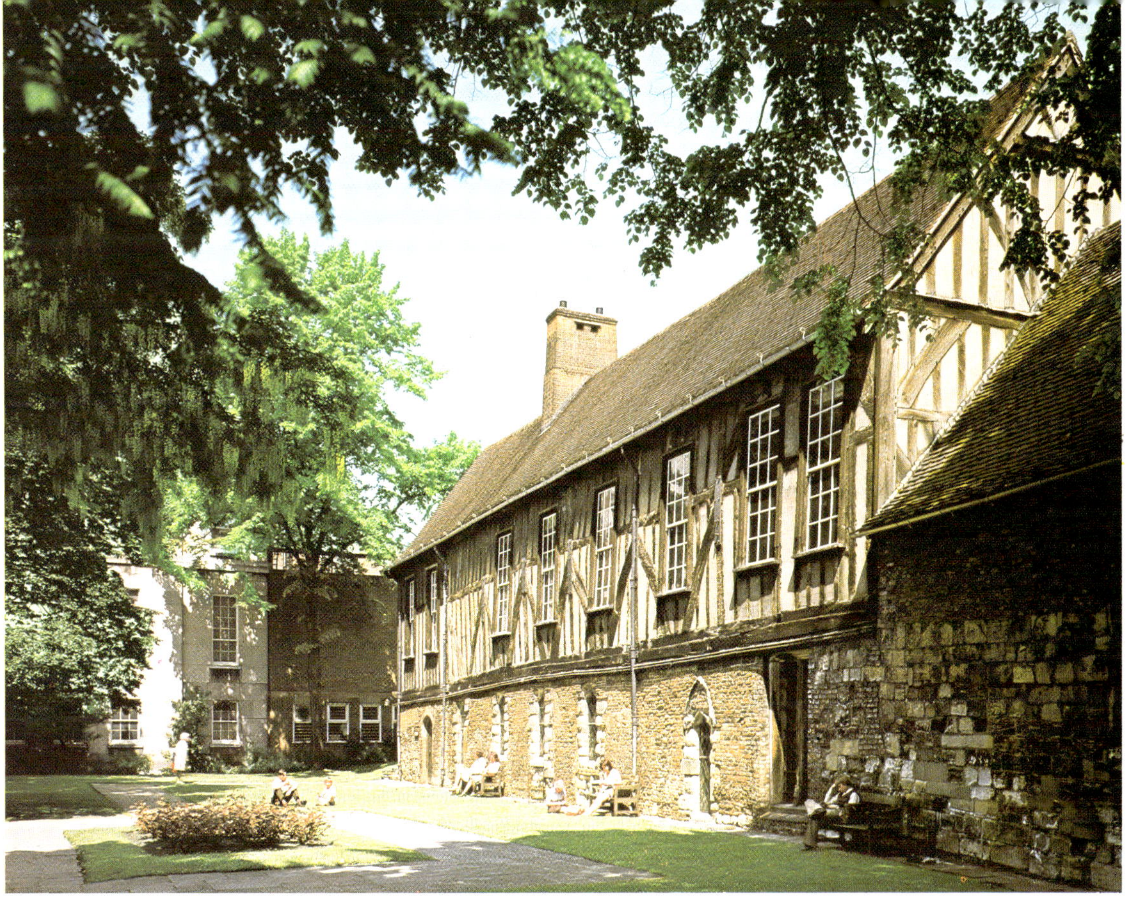

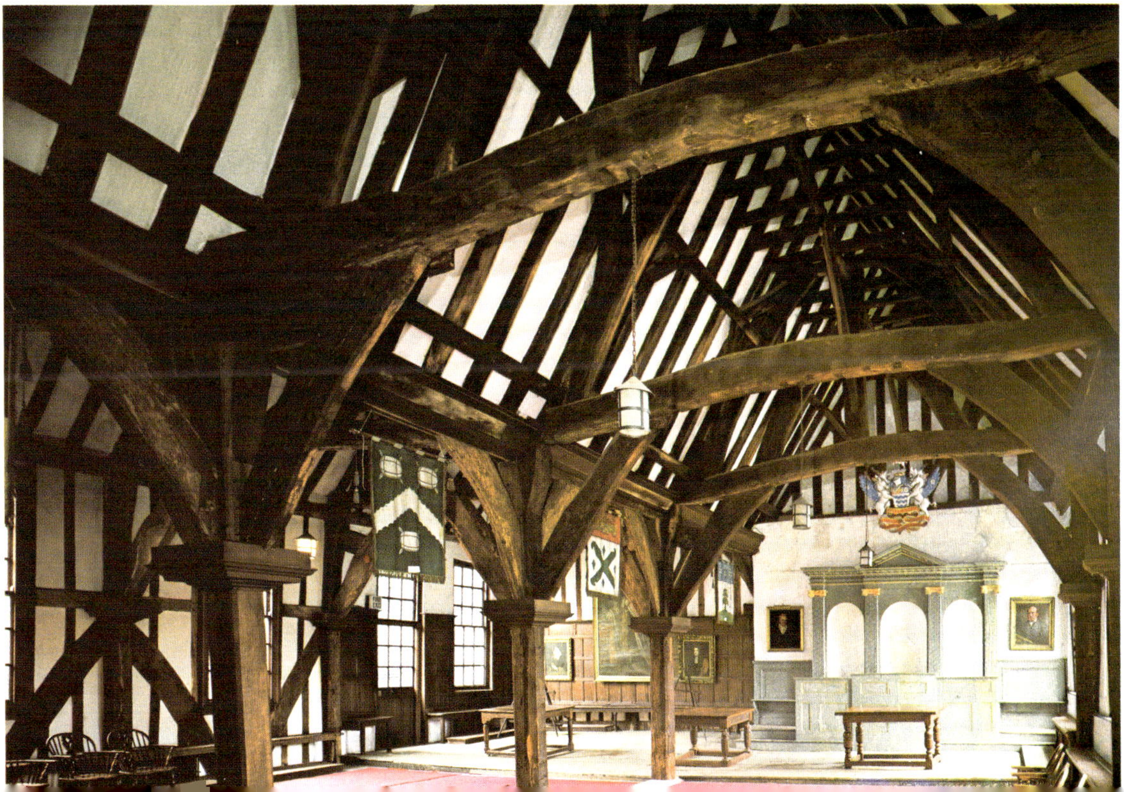

south to campaign in Wessex against Alfred and on returning to the city in 876 their leader, Halfdene, was given the title of the first Danish king of York.

The palace of the Danish kings was situated at the north end of the Shambles in what is now known as King's Court. The name of the capital was changed from Eoforwic to Jorvik; this was pronounced Yorwik and later became York. Trade expanded and the population grew and this independent kingdom prospered for some 50 years.

The Danish kings of York were bitter enemies of king Alfred and it is possible that Danish ships sailed down the Ouse to join others in harassing the West Saxons.

As time passed, Athelstan of Wessex annexed Danish Northumbria to the crown of England; this happened in 926 and a year later he drove the Danes out of the city altogether, proclaiming himself king of all Britain. After another battle in 937 in which Athelstan was again victorious, he founded St. Peter's Hospital, later to be rededicated to St. Leonard, the ruins of which are in the Museum Gardens.

The next episode in the story of York was a prelude to events which were to completely change the history of England.

In 1055 Tostig, the son of earl Godwin, was made earl of all Northumbria, but some ten years later, after an insurrection, he was outlawed. At this time, Edward the Confessor was king of England, and on his death he was succeeded by Harold Godwinson, earl of Wessex. It was some time, however, before the unruly Northumbrians accepted Harold as king. Tostig, having allied himself with Harold Hardrada, the Norwegian king, ravaged the coast and after landing near York won a great battle and entered the city.

Harold Hardrada now saw himself as king of England and after reprovisioning the army he withdrew from the city to wait for hostages before proceeding southwards. Instead of hostages arriving, Harold Godwinson came with his army. Having hurried from the south he caught Tostig and Hardrada completely by surprise and in the terrible battle that followed almost all the invaders were annihilated.

However, while Harold Godwinson was in York, news came that England had been invaded by William of Normandy. The English army at once rushed south to meet the invader and on the 14 October 1066 Harold was killed, his army defeated and William of Normandy became king of England.

York by this time had become a

\* \* \*

ABOVE: *A view of the East end of the Minster from College Street.*

FACING PAGE (above): *Clifford's Tower is the medieval keep of York Castle. In 1068 William the Conqueror erected a castle on each side of the river. All that remains of the castle on the west side is the mound on which it stood.*

FACING PAGE (below): *Micklegate Bar is the gateway through which the monarch traditionally enters the city.*

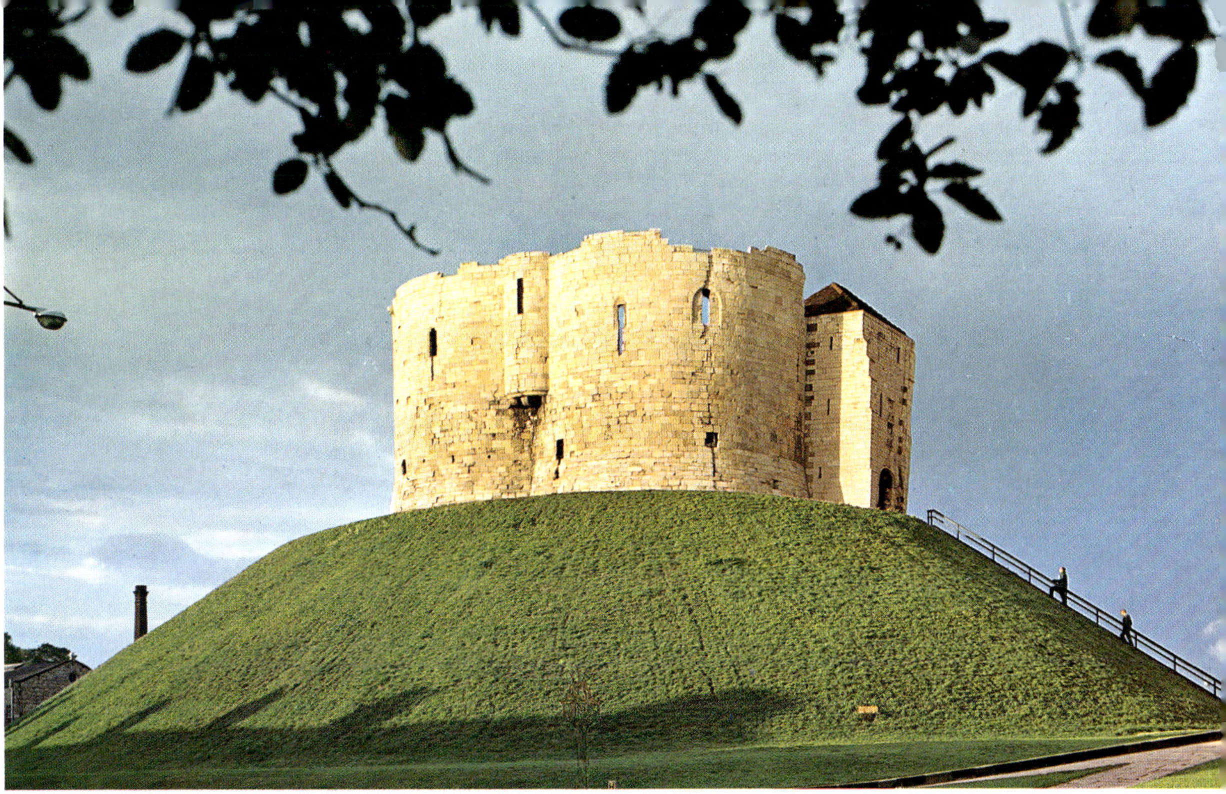

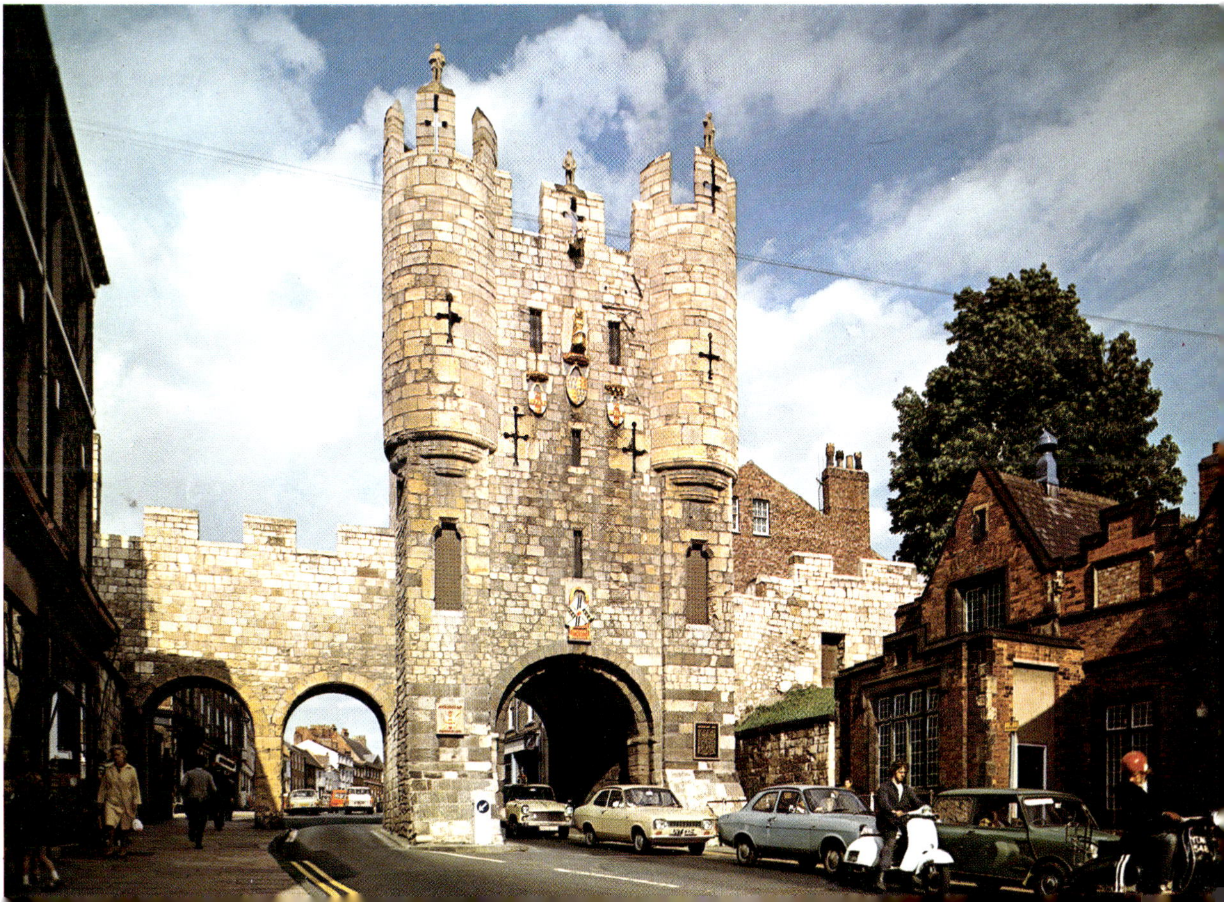

thriving and prosperous city. Its narrow streets were lined with houses which looked much as the Shambles appears today. This street is about 1000 years old and the Domesday Book records that count de Mortain had in the city of York 14 mansions, two stalls in the Shambles and the church of St. Crux. All the properties in the Shambles have been restored and today play a full and thriving part in the commerce of the city. Some of the half-timbered gables overhang in successive stages until at the uppermost level, by leaning out of a window, you can almost reach across to the property opposite. Newgate Market which was formed out of the rear of the Shambles echoes the bustling activities of earlier times.

When the Romans left the city, Eboracum covered 52 acres, but by Norman times York was five times this size.

William took possession of York and built a fortified position or castle on the mound of the old Danish stronghold where Clifford's Tower now stands. After he had left, an attack was made on the city by Atheling who came down from Scotland with his supporters. The inhabitants allowed the attackers to enter the city, but word reached the Conqueror, who returned, retook the city and put many to the sword.

After William had returned to Winchester, another disastrous attack was made, this time by the Danes in 1069. On this occasion the Norman garrison was heavily defeated but it was not long before the Conqueror once again returned and this time he laid waste to much of the city and to large areas of the north country. For many years there was utter desolation in the north. The castle was repaired, but it was not until about 1245 (by which time the keep was known as Clifford's Tower) that rebuilding in stone took place.

Just before the Norman occupation, except for the marshy land between Fossgate and the Red Tower, York was surrounded by a mound of earth which was surmounted by a timber stockade. The Normans probably built arches into these mounds where the roads passed through and these arches were the beginnings of the four medieval gateways, Micklegate, Monk, Walmgate and Bootham Bars, all of which still exist. It was through Micklegate Bar that the king traditionally entered the city, and one of the earliest references to the bars occurred in 1196 when permission was given to erect a house on or near this bar. Monk Bar and Walmgate Bar covered the roads to and from the sea. Bootham Bar was the entrance from the north, through the forest of Galtres. Armed guards were stationed at Bootham Bar to conduct travellers through the forest and protect them from wolves. In the 14th century each bar had a drawbridge and a barbican to protect the gate. Only the barbican of Walmgate Bar now remains.

The boundaries of the city were, by this time, roughly as they are today and, outside the walls, houses had been built on each side of the roads for the distance of about a mile.

York began to recover its greatness when William Rufus was king. It was a time of much rebuilding in stone and St. Mary's Abbey which had been founded about 1088 was greatly enlarged. The nearby hospital of St. Leonard was rebuilt in about 1142 by king Stephen.

An interesting group of shops is to be seen in Goodramgate and these probably form one of the oldest rows of property in York. In order to endow a chantry of the Virgin Mary the

*Continued on page 14*

★ ★ ★

LEFT: *St. Mary's Abbey. The first monastic house to be established in Yorkshire after the Norman Conquest, St. Mary's became one of the largest and wealthiest of the Benedictine order. It was suppressed in 1540 during the dissolution of the monasteries.*

FACING PAGE (top left): *The south transept of York Minster was built between 1220–40 by archbishop Walter de Grey.*

FACING PAGE (top right): *Low Petergate stands on the old Roman* via principalis.

FACING PAGE (below): *The Norman crypt, the oldest part of the Minster, and traditionally the place where Edwin, king of Northumbria, was baptised in A.D. 627. The Romanesque carvings on the capitals are especially fine.*

10

ABOVE: *The High Altar, York Minster.* FACING PAGE: *The medieval Shambles, once the butchers' quarter of York.*

parishioners of Holy Trinity Church agreed in 1316 to the building of some property once known as Our Lady's Row. These houses which were built in front of the church are now in use as shops. The church itself contains some fine stained glass, box pews and a squint. The list of rectors dates from the 13th century but the church is of older foundation.

York was the seat of Parliament in 1332, 1333, 1335 and 1336, and when war broke out with the Scots in 1333 king Edward III put himself at the head of his army leaving his queen, Philippa, in York. Later, when he was at war in France, Philippa again came to York; this time she gathered an army herself and put the Scots to flight.

The first reference to the mayor of York was made during the reign of Stephen and it seems to have been an established office by that time. In 1389 when Richard II came to York to settle a dispute, he took the sword from his side and presented it to the mayor declaring that the title of Lord Mayor was bestowed on him and his successors for ever. Later, in 1396, York was granted a charter which allowed the sword to be carried point uppermost in the presence of all the noblemen of England. In the same year the title of the duke of York was created, and the city became independent of the county.

Trade with Germany and the low countries during the early part of the 13th century brought wealth to the city and the trades Gilds grew in importance. Some of these were of very early foundation. The forerunner of York's most famous medieval Gild, the Fellowship of Mercers and Merchant Adventurers, existed in the time of king Stephen and perhaps earlier.

Corpus Christi Day was introduced into England in about 1325 and by 1372 both the festival and the pageant were observed in York. They were very popular and Richard II made several special journeys to attend them. Each Gild took a prominent part in the pageant and enacted a story taken from the Bible: the Tanners took part in the creation, the Mariners in the story of Noah's Ark and so on.

These plays, named Mystery Plays, were performed in set places and Toft Green was the one appointed for assembly before the start of the procession. The stages were constructed in tiers and on wheels so that they could be drawn round to various parts of the city. The acting took place on the upper tier while the lower section was screened round and used as a dressing room. The plays were always popular and a good deal of discontent followed when they were discontinued. The Mystery Plays are now the centrepiece of the York Festival which takes place every third year and they are performed in front of the lovely ruins of St. Mary's Abbey.

Most of the Gilds had a hall and a chapel; the hall of the powerful Gild of the Merchant Adventurers was built about 1361 and is situated between Piccadilly and Fossgate. Another Gild was that of St. Anthony. In the middle of the 14th century the Gild of the Lord's Prayer was a very powerful force in the City and in 1447 the members took over St. Anthony's Hall in Peasholme Green and rebuilt it. Various changes took place over the years and in 1705 part of the hall became the Blue Coat School. Today this delightful building is used by the University of York.

The finest hall is the Guildhall and it is approached along a passage by the side of the Mansion House. It was built by the Gild of St. Christopher in

* * *

LEFT: *The Mansion House was built in 1725-6 to serve as the Lord Mayor's residence during his year of office. It has an imposing state room and a valuable collection of antique silver plate.*

FACING PAGE (above): *The King's Manor. Built as a residence for the Abbot of St. Mary's, it later became the headquarters of the King's Council in the north. It is now used by the university.*

FACING PAGE (below): *St. William's College founded in 1461 for the chantry priests of the cathedral. It is now used by the Convocation of York.*

14

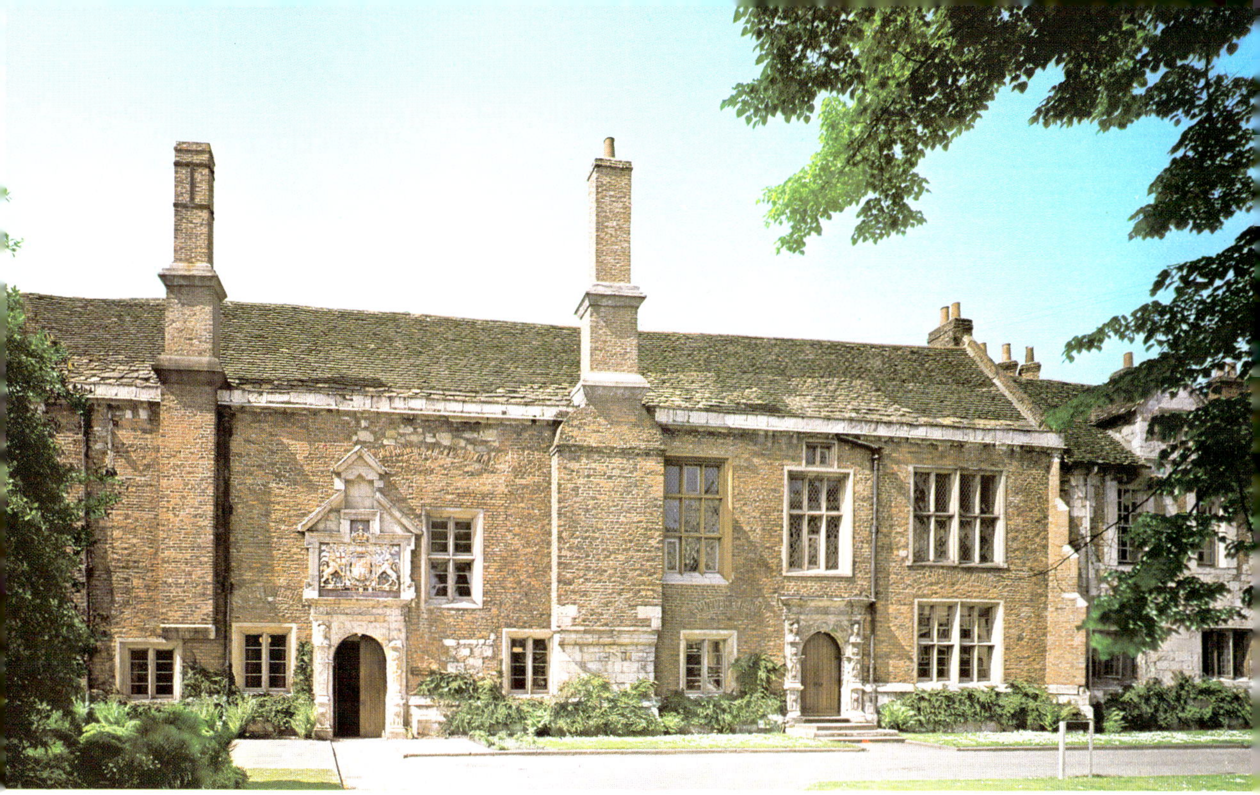

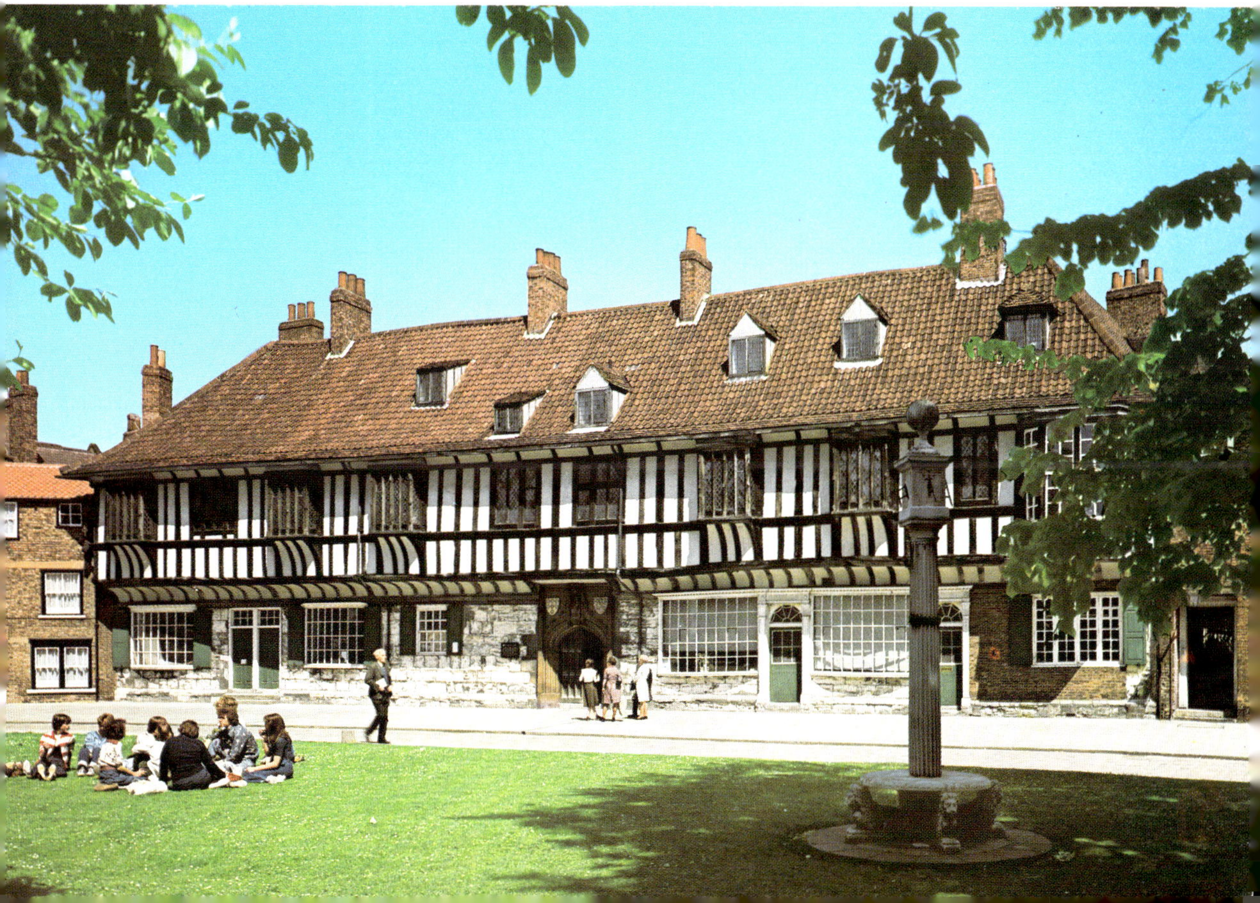

co-operation with the Common Council between 1449 and 1459. It was in the beautiful panelled committee room at the end of the hall that in 1648 £200,000 was paid to the Scottish army for the capture of the king.

The Guildhall was badly damaged by enemy action during the Second World War, but it was restored shortly afterwards. Several tokens of friendship with York's twin town, Munster, can be seen in the Guildhall.

During the reigns of Edward IV and Richard III York was at the highest peak of influence since Norman times. Edward IV was crowned king in the almost completed Minster in 1464. After the battle of Hexham the heads of his vanquished enemies were, in accordance with custom, displayed on Micklegate Bar.

After Richard III came to the throne he visited York on many occasions and was always welcomed with loyalty and pageantry. With his death on the battlefield of Bosworth the Middle Ages came to an end.

The Minster was completed, almost as it can be seen today, in 1472.

Edwin, king of Northumbria, was baptised on Easter Eve in 627 along with his Druid priests in a small timber church on the site of the Roman *praetorium*. Soon afterwards work on a small church of stone was commenced but before it was complete Edwin was killed and it was not until 669, when Wilfrid became bishop of York, that work was restarted on the cathedral. This Minster had taken about 42 years to complete. Alcuin records that a new lofty church was built at York with strong columns, carved arches, fine windows and roof,

and was consecrated by bishop Albert in 781.

About 300 years after this date, when the city was under attack, the Norman garrison, thinking that some buildings near to the Minster might give cover to the insurgents, set fire to the property and the flames spread to the Minster, destroying it along with the library. This occurred in 1069 and the loss of books and

\* \* \*

ABOVE: *The National Railway Museum, York, was opened by the Duke of Edinburgh on 27 September 1975. It is part of the Science Museum, London, and contains over 20 full-size locomotives, several carriages, and show-cases on the technical, economic and social development of the railways.*

16

ABOVE: *One of the reconstructed streets in the Castle Folk Museum, founded to house the collections of bygones of Dr. J. L. Kirk. The shop fronts were carefully preserved from demolished buildings in York and they represent a variety of trades. The cobbled street is complete with hansom cab.*

records was immeasurable not only to York but the whole country.

Thomas of Bayeux became archbishop in 1070 and shortly afterwards he reorganised the administration of the church and commenced the rebuilding of the Minster. The church of Thomas Bayeux was damaged by fire in 1137, it was repaired some time between 1154 and 1181 and the choir was rebuilt.

\* \* \*

Except for parts of the cathedral which can be seen in the crypt and for some other fragments, the earliest part of the Minster which can be seen today is the south transept. This was started about 1227 by archbishop de Grey who had the vision of a larger and more magnificent cathedral. It is in the Early English style and the south elevation, viewed from the Minster gates is amongst the finest of its period which can be seen anywhere. Work on the north aisle was carried out between 1245 and 1260.

The Minster is a treasure house of glass and amongst the most beautiful is the grisaille glass in the five Early English lancets which form the Five Sisters' Window at the end of the north transept.

Some 25 years after the work on the north transept was completed, work was commenced on the chapter house and the result is a wonderful achievement of construction and beauty. The windows which belong to the decorated period indicate that the chapter house could not have been completed much before 1340. So highly was the chapter house thought of that inscribed on it are the words "as the rose is the flower of flowers so is this the house of houses".

Archbishop Romeyn commenced the rebuilding of the nave in 1291. At this stage the choir which had been constructed some 200 years earlier by archbishop Roger was out of proportion with the remainder of the cathedral and in 1361 it was decided that it should be rebuilt on the same magnificent scale as the nave. The Zouche Chapel was built in 1340 and work on the great perpendicular cen-

17

TOP: *The De Grey Rooms which were erected in St. Leonard's Place in about 1842 and named after earl de Grey were intended primarily to house the officers' mess of the Yorkshire Hussars. The Department of Tourism now occupy part of the building.*

ABOVE: *The Theatre Royal built about 1750 on the site of St. Leonard's Hospital, was rebuilt in 1765. A new elevation to St. Leonard's Place was constructed in 1835. The foyer of glass and concrete was added in 1967.*

FACING PAGE (above): *Guildhall Reach. The 15th-century Guildhall seen from the south side of the river. It was built in 1449–59 by the city and the Gild of St. Christopher and St. George.*

FACING PAGE (below): *The Castle Museum which was opened in 1938. Originally the prison for females built in 1780 by John Carr, a York architect, it now houses a famous collection of folk life. The Debtors' Prison built in 1705 also forms part of this unique collection.*

tral tower was commenced in 1405. On 3 July 1472 a solemn service was held to reconsecrate the completed Minster.

Great damage was caused in 1829 when a fire was started by a fanatic which burned down the roof of the choir and chancel. Restoration work took three years to complete and late in 1840 the bells crashed down to the floor, when the roof of the south-west tower was badly damaged by another fire. The bells were replaced in 1844 and Big Peter, the huge bell weighing over 12 tons first rang out in August 1845. Big Peter rings out daily at noon.

The story of the Minster is in many ways like that of the City, one of change, rebuilding, the introduction of new ideas and of excellence in art and craft.

King Richard's close association with York caused the city a good deal of apprehension after his defeat at Bosworth, but fears were dispelled when Henry VII's messenger announced that the king "greeted the city well."

After the Pilgrimage of Grace had been put down with much severity, on the orders of Henry VIII, the King's Council in the north was re-established at York in 1537. The house of the abbot of St. Mary's Abbey was used by the council and a new house was erected nearer to the river for the use of the king when visiting York, but only fragments of this later building remain.

The first monastic establishment to be suppressed in York was St. Clement's Nunnery. This occurred in 1535 and the last prioress retired to live in a house which still stands in Trinity Lane. It later became an inn bearing the name of Jacob's Well but eventually it was altered and is now used as the hall of Holy Trinity Church Micklegate. The Act of 1539 brought dissolution to other monastic institutions including St. Mary's Abbey and St. Leonard's Hospital.

It was during queen Elizabeth's reign in 1570 that Guy Fawkes was baptized in St. Michael the Belfrey Church. He was born in a house in Petergate nearby and was educated at St. Peter's School.

The 16th century saw a great change in the commercial life of the city. York had been a city of international business fame, but by the end of the century most of its trade had been lost to London.

When the Civil War broke out, the

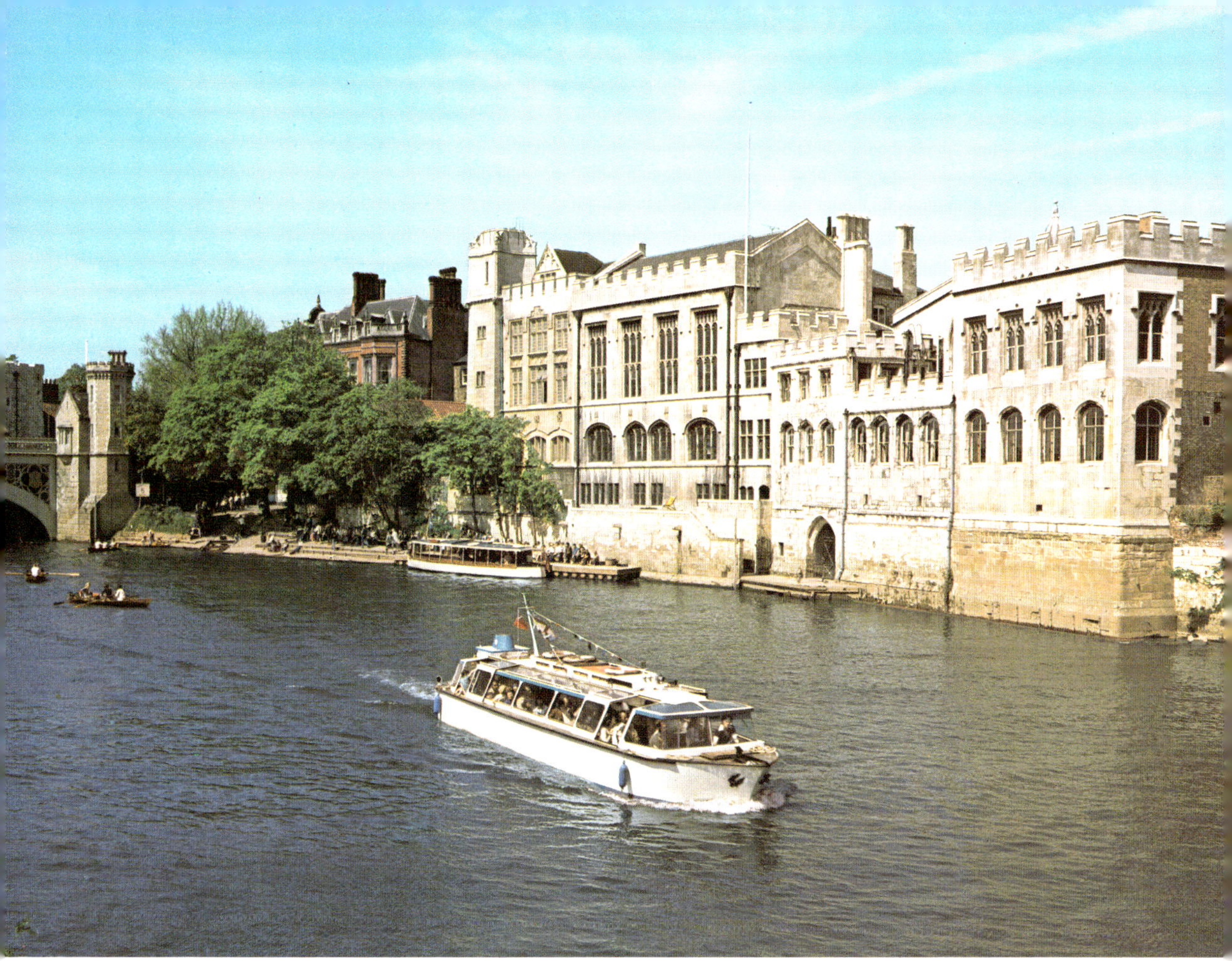

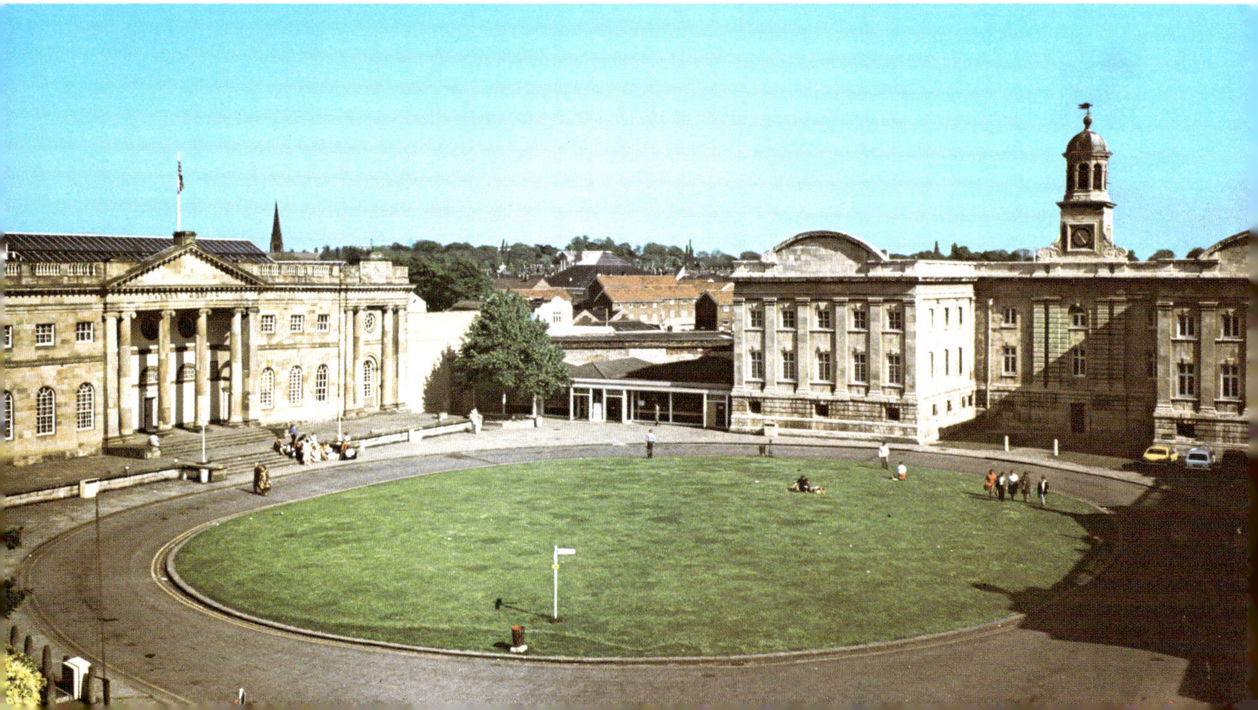

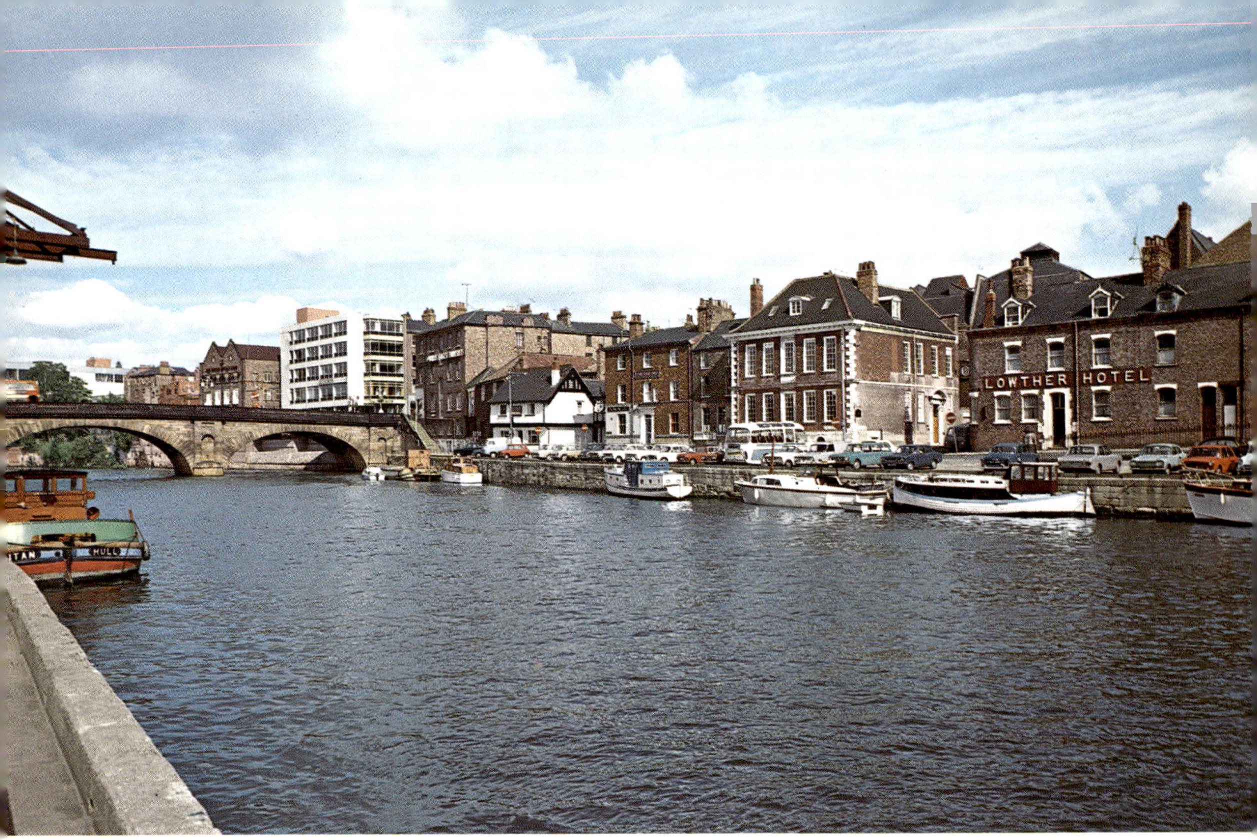
LOWTHER HOTEL
HULL

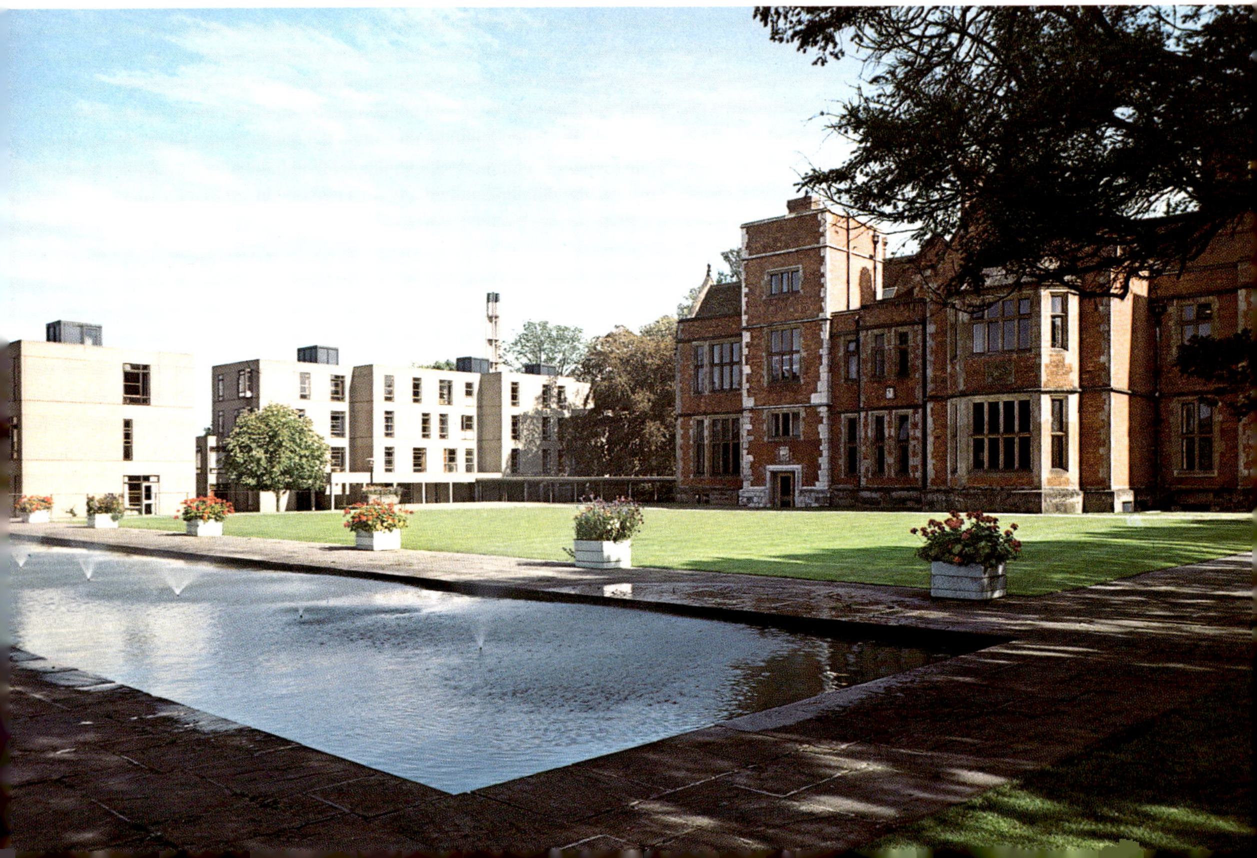

city was besieged early in 1644, and although the siege was raised for a short time after the Royalist defeat at Marston Moor, York was again surrounded. Several churches were destroyed and the tower of St. Olave's Church which was used as an artillery platform, suffered a good deal of damage. In June 1644 St. Mary's Tower in Marygate was also damaged and when the abbey walls were breached, the insurgents fought their way across to the King's Manor but were driven out. After a desperate resistance the Royalists surrendered honourably on fair terms and marched out of the city. This stirring period ended with a service of Thanksgiving in the Minster.

Early in the 18th century, any disused building of stone construction however ancient, was considered to be a 'quarry' and in 1705 much of St. Mary's Abbey was removed and used to repair St. Olave's Church which had fallen into disrepair. Similarly between 1701 and 1705 stone from the abbey was used in the rebuilding of a new prison near Clifford's Tower. The Debtors' Prison, as it was named, was designed by Sir John Vanbrugh and it was referred to by Daniel Defoe as "the most stately most complete prison in the whole kingdom." Felons were kept in part of the prison and Dick Turpin, the notorious highwayman, was imprisoned there in 1739.

Stage coach travel from York to London began in 1703; journeys could be undertaken on Mondays, Wednesdays and Fridays between the Black Swan in Holborn, London, and the Black Swan in Coney Street, York.

York greatly increased in importance as a social centre in the 18th century. Horse racing, which had taken place on the Ings at Clifton

\* \* \*

FACING PAGE (above): *The King's Staith, on the east side of the Ouse, has from ancient times been a place bustling with commercial activity.*

FACING PAGE (below): *Part of the University of York, at Heslington. The modern buildings contrast attractively with the mellow brickwork of the Hall which houses the administrative staff.*

RIGHT: *The interior of the Guildhall. Much of it was destroyed by fire in the Second World War and restoration was completed in 1960.*

from the 16th century, was reintroduced in 1709 and about this time ladies and gentlemen of the county met each Monday to play cards and dance. Their first meeting place was the King's Manor. Then they met at a house in Minster Yard and finally in the Assembly Rooms which were specially built for this purpose. The building was designed by the earl of Burlington in the Renaissance style, the foundation stone being laid in 1731.

At this time Davygate and Stonegate joined together in front of the Mansion House and by 1743 the burial ground of the beautiful little church of St. Helen had become so raised by successive interments that it was necessary to go up steps to the burial ground and down again into the church. In order to give better access to the Assembly Rooms the burial ground was removed in 1745. The list of rectors of St. Helen goes back to the 13th century but the church, which was fortunately saved from demolition in 1547, is of much older foundation.

During the 18th century the beauty of the city was further enhanced by many delightful new buildings. One of these was the Mansion House which was built in 1726 probably to the design or advice of the earl of Burlington. Attempts had been made to purchase the Red House in Duncombe Place for use as the residence of the Lord Mayor but as these were unsuccessful the Mansion House with its elegant state room was erected.

The Assize Courts designed in the Ionic style by the noted York architect, John Carr, were completed in 1777 and opposite to them the Female Prison was constructed in 1780. Dr. John L. Kirk, a medical practitioner of Pickering near York, gave his unique folk collection to the city and in 1938 the Female Prison and the Debtors' Prison adjoining it were adapted and opened as the Castle Museum. Dr. Kirk's collection was the nucleus of the exhibits in the museum. Whole streets of shops, houses, cottages and work places have been reconstructed and contain a wealth of fascinating material. The museum really *lives* and without doubt is amongst the finest of its kind to be found anywhere.

The Red House was built in the early 18th century in Duncombe Place and stands on the site of what was once the gatehouse of St. Leonard's Hospital. Next to it stands the Theatre Royal. Theatrical productions were first performed in an old room in the Minster Yard but these were discontinued in 1741. About 9 years later, Joseph Baker built a small theatre and in 1765 the larger and more elegant Theatre Royal was constructed. The original entrance to the Theatre was in Duncombe Place but when in 1835 the Corporation formed the dignified crescent of St. Leonard's Place an entrance was formed giving access to the theatre from the new street. Part of the city wall was removed so that the development could be carried out.

The elegant De Grey Rooms were built in 1842 in St. Leonard's Place, and opposite, in the Italian style, the Art Gallery was built in 1879 as part of the Great York Exhibition. It contains many fine works of art including those of the famous York artist William Etty.

Nearby in the historic Museum

\* \* \*

LEFT: *The Assembly Rooms were built in 1731 and designed by the earl of Burlington.*

FACING PAGE (above left): *The site of All Saints Pavement was a place of worship before the Conquest. The Norman church was rebuilt in the 15th century. A lantern in the tower was a guide to travellers.*

FACING PAGE (above right): *The spire of St Mary's Church, Castlegate, which was recorded in the Domesday Book, now converted into a heritage centre housing 'The York Story', a fine exhibition in pictures, models and sound.*

FACING PAGE (below left): *Our Lady's Row, Goodramgate. In 1316 the parishioners of Holy Trinity Church agreed to the building of Our Lady's Row so that a chantry to the Virgin Mary could be endowed.*

FACING PAGE (below right): *St. Martin's Church, Coney Street. Built in the 15th century, this fine old church was all but destroyed in an air raid in 1942. Only the south aisle survived and from this a shrine of Remembrance was created.*

23

Gardens the Yorkshire Philosophical Society built the Yorkshire Museum, which was opened to the public in February 1830. The museum houses many remarkable remains of Roman origin and other collections of great interest. The Hospitium which was originally the guest house of St. Mary's Abbey also has Roman material on display.

Close by the church of St. Mary Castlegate, in which the living story of York can be seen, is Fairfax House, which dates from 1755. It is a fine building of national importance and has been restored to house a remarkable collection of furniture and clocks.

\* \* \*

ABOVE: *The Jorvik Viking Centre, Coppergate. The importance of the Viking city of Jorvik was revealed in the excavations at Coppergate, begun in 1976. A remarkable collection of 10th-century remains was uncovered, including houses and workshops still containing tools, cooking utensils, jewellery and shoes. The buildings were reconstructed exactly where they were found and within six months of the Centre's opening in April 1984 over half a million visitors had already taken the most exciting journey in a thousand years through the busy wharf, market and dark smoky houses. Here a ship from Norway is moored on the banks of the river Foss while its cargo of skins, wine and herring is unloaded.*

There are many more fine buildings to be seen in York, such as Micklegate House; Cumberland House; St. George's House, Castlegate; and the graceful Georgian houses in Bootham. This was certainly a period of excellence and delicacy in architecture which has not been surpassed.

New trade sprang up in the early part of the 19th century including chocolate making, flour milling and tanning, the glass industry, insurance and banking. The opening of the railway from Stockton to Darlington quickly led to further developments and the York and North Midland Railway Company was formed in York in 1835 by George Hudson, the 'Railway King', a local linen draper.

York is now the home of the National Railway Museum which opened in September 1975 and had its millionth visitor in April 1976. The oldest locomotive on display is 'Agenoria' dating from 1829, but perhaps the most famous is 'Mallard' which in 1938 set up a still unbroken world speed record for steam locomotives.

Trading activities continued to flourish and advances were made in the field of general education.

The famous Rowntree family of chocolate manufacturers played a large part in improving the general welfare and adult education of the people of the city. Seebohm Rowntree's first great success, his book *Poverty, a Study of Town Life*, published in 1901, was quickly recognised as a work of immense social importance; and the Joseph Rowntree village is practical evidence of the family's concern for the people of York.

In April 1960 approval for the establishment of a university was obtained and York, which has been in the forefront of educational activity since the 7th century at last gained a university of its own. It stands in an estate of about 190 acres at Heslington, some two miles outside the city. The administrative headquarters are in Heslington Hall, a house of Elizabethan origin which was rebuilt in the 19th century. The new buildings are of striking design. Some have been formed round an artificial lake and are linked by covered ways.

Today the people of York are aware that the city is again passing through a period of change, but that awareness will ensure that the character and beauty of this city, where change and danger have always been constant companions, will be conserved for the future.

### ACKNOWLEDGMENTS

All the photographs are by Gerald Newbery, FIIP, FRPS; except pp. 1, 4, 5, 9, 13, 17, 20 and 21 by Pickards of Leeds; p. 16 by National Railway Museum, crown copyright reserved; p. 23 (top right) by York Castle Museum; p. 24 by Douglas Unwin.

ISBN 0 85372 144 0